# ROCK & ROLL
## HALL OF FAMERS

# David Bowie

## THOMAS FORGET

the rosen publishing group's
**rosen
central**

*To all the pretty things*

Published in 2002 by The Rosen Publishing Group, Inc.

29 East 21st Street, New York, NY 10010

Copyright © 2002 by The Rosen Publishing Group, Inc.

First Edition

**Library of Congress Cataloging-in-Publication Data**

Forget, Thomas.

David Bowie/by Thomas Forget.— 1st ed.

p. cm. — (Rock & roll hall of famers)

Includes discography, filmography, list of Web sites, bibliographical references, and index.

ISBN 0-8239-3523-X (library binding)

1. Bowie, David—Juvenile literature. 2. Rock musicians—England—Biography—Juvenile literature. [1. Bowie, David. 2. Musicians. 3. Rock music.] I. Title. II. Series.

ML3930.B68 F67 2002

782.42166'092–dc21

2001003821

*Manufactured in the United States of America*

# CONTENTS

David Bowie is an innovator who has entertained music fans for more than three decades.

# Introduction

David Bowie gave the rock and roll world a much-needed blood transfusion in the 1970s. When David first gained popularity, no one had seen anything like him before. His unique look, which included makeup, wildly colored hair, and outrageous costumes, shocked many audiences and made people stand up and take notice of his equally interesting music. While many rock artists had used costumes and fashion as a part of their act, no one in

David Bowie, pictured here onstage, has always blurred the lines between music, film, and theater.

music had ever done it quite like David Bowie. The many characters he created for the stage blurred the lines between music, film, and theater. "I am an actor," David has said. "My whole professional life is an act. I slip from one guise to another very easily. One guise plays into another, and the extreme comments force it into another direction."

Even without costumes, David Bowie continues to thrill his audiences with his willingness to try things that are completely different. Unlike so many rockers before him, he has never been afraid to completely change his style. He has been a folk singer, a straight-ahead rocker, a soul singer, a disco artist, and a pioneer of electronic and techno music. Despite all these changes in his style, the public has remained interested in him and his music. Because he has succeeded in so many different styles of music, it is almost impossible to find a popular artist today that has not been influenced by David Bowie.

Bowie has also become a real supporter of the Internet. He was one of the first artists to develop a personal Web site. He even made himself a publicly owned company, selling stock in his career. Because he is so willing to change and grow with the times, there are a number of young, modern musicians, including Nine Inch Nails and the Smashing Pumpkins, who have recorded and played music with him.

Throughout his long career, he has had a number of top twenty albums and singles in the United States, and has regularly dominated the charts in Britain. He has produced and written hit albums with well-known musicians, such as Lou Reed and Iggy Pop. He's a talented painter. He has acted in films by famous directors, such as Martin Scorsese and David Lynch. He has even played the Elephant Man on Broadway. His different personas, such as Ziggy Stardust, the Thin White Duke, and Aladdin Sane, have kept his fans interested and excited in his music. By constantly reinventing himself, his career has outlasted many of the people that started in music at the same time.

Today, David Bowie is a member of the exclusive club of Rock and Roll Hall of Fame inductees, but he is not happy to rest on past achievements. He continues making music and art, and he remains an exciting performer.

# David Robert Jones

While David Bowie is the name that we all know him by, it is not the name he was born with. David Robert Jones was born on January 8, 1947, to John, a press agent for a charity organization, and his wife Peggy, a former waitress. David's mother previously had two children by two different fathers (one boy named Terry and a girl given up for adoption whom David never met), but he was his parents' first child together and they always favored him over Terry.

John and Peggy's first home together was in a very poor neighborhood in north London. They moved to Brixton, a slightly better neighborhood, as soon as they could. Things were always hard for the Jones family, as they had very little money, but David's parents always spoiled him as much as their money would allow. When David was nine, his half brother Terry moved in with the family. Terry had been living with Peggy's mother, but she was starting to show signs of mental illness and Terry could no longer be left in her care. Terry also loved little David very much and spent as much time with him as possible. John and Peggy Jones were uncomfortable with Terry, because he reminded them of their past mistakes and failed romances. This forced Terry to turn to David for the love that was missing in his life. Terry would eventually be the person who introduced David to the world of music. Terry was a huge jazz fan and brought David into the big city of London for the first time.

David's father was very interested in show business and even owned a nightclub when he was younger. John became a press agent for a charity organization and often got to meet celebrities that did benefit performances. He would always introduce David to the celebrities he met. John Jones wanted his son to be an entertainer. He was willing to do whatever it took to help his son reach this goal.

In 1956, Terry left for a tour of duty in Britain's Royal Air Force (RAF). That same year, Elvis Presley exploded onto the English pop charts with an amazing six hits in the top twenty. David loved Elvis and was especially impressed with how many different personalities Elvis presented in his songs. Seeing how interested his son was in music, and in Elvis in particular, John bought David a ukulele (a small strumming guitar), and helped him build a string bass guitar.

## Private Schoolhouse Rock

In 1957, David's family moved again, this time to Bromley, a middle-class neighborhood in

England. The following autumn, David started high school at Bromley Technical High School. Bromley Tech was typical of many English high schools, as it was mostly geared towards preparing the students for one specific career that they would study throughout their four years. David entered the "art stream," which specialized in preparing and training students for careers in commercial art. David was a very average student in class and was not very interested in his studies. He was, however, becoming more and more fascinated with music. Terry had returned from the RAF, and while David's mother and father did not allow him to live with them, he visited David often. Terry brought him to jazz clubs in London, where they listened to the best jazz musicians of the time, including Terry's favorite saxophonist, Ronnie Ross.

John Jones had bought David a white plastic saxophone, and David decided to call Ronnie Ross for saxophone lessons. Ross gave David the lessons for four months, and David kept it secret from his classmates. When he was

The saxophone, Bowie's first instrument, remains a vital part of his musical repertoire.

finished with the lessons, there were many stories going around his school that he was already a good sax player, without anyone having heard him play. It seemed that David had already learned how to cause a sensation, and he enjoyed being talked about. Since he liked the feeling of being the subject of gossip so much, he continued to do interesting things that would set him apart from the rest of his schoolmates. When he had a school assignment to make a business card, he put the name "Luther J." on his, causing a buzz among the other students. This would be the first of many aliases for David Jones. Encouraged by the kids' reaction to his individuality, David started to do other outrageous things, like putting an orange streak in his hair and styling it in an imitation of the styles worn by American rockers, such as Elvis Presley and Little Richard.

## Fun Fact!

David Bowie has eyes that appear to be two different colors. The truth is that as a result of a fight with a schoolmate, one of his eyes was badly damaged. David's right pupil is stuck in the open position, which makes it look very different from his left one. The strange eyes contribute to David's alien look.

14

# The British Invasion Reaches America

In 1962, an English band called the Rolling Stones made their debut, and another band called the Beatles started to become popular. Up until this time, American rock and roll had dominated all of the charts. Suddenly it seemed possible for English boys to make popular music that the whole world could hear. When the Beatles released "Love Me Do," David was the first person in his class to own the single, and he memorized the harmonica part played by John Lennon.

In an instant, England had become the center of the rock and roll universe, and every young man in the country wanted to be in on the action. David was no exception. Soon, David and his friend George Underwood formed a band, calling themselves the Konrads. David sang and played the saxophone. He loved the attention that he got from playing music. In fact, when a teacher asked what he wanted to be when he graduated, David told him, "I want to be a pop idol." It was the same kind of grand statement that David would later build his impressive career on, and it showed just how confident he was that he had what it took to be a star. It also showed that he understood publicity and that shocking people was the perfect way to stir up interest. His teacher and classmates were the first to be outraged, but it would only be a matter of time before he would stun the world and meet his unusual career goals. First, however, there was a lot of work to be done for young David Jones.

## The Man in the Band

Once David graduated from high school, he landed a job as a junior commercial artist at the Design Group, Ltd. There, he helped prepare advertisements for print and set type. While David loved art, he didn't enjoy doing it for advertising. He wanted to do something truly creative, not just help to sell products. He was still playing music and had a new band

# Early Taste of Fame

Despite not being interested in sports, David was so obsessed with America when he was young that he wrote the United States embassy in England for any and all information they had on American football. They replied with an invitation to the embassy and gave him a football uniform and ball. Photos were taken and sent to American and British newspapers with captions such as "Limey Kid Digs Football."

called Davie Jones and the King Bees, in which he was the lead singer and saxophone player. The British pop craze was in full swing and every young musician in England dreamt of being in the next Beatles or Rolling Stones, the two most successful groups at the time. Because the Beatles had a manager, John Jones believed that David's band needed a manager to help them as well. With his help, David began writing letters to successful businessmen asking them to help finance his band and buy them new equipment.

One letter, written to a washing machine manufacturer, ended up in the hands of a talent scout for Dick James, the Beatles' music publisher. Soon, Davie Jones and the King Bees found themselves auditioning for Decca Records, the same label that the Rolling Stones were on. They passed the audition, and Decca recorded a single, "Liza Jane," released in June of 1964. Unfortunately, this quick taste of success did not last, as the record was a flop. Like many of the other young bands, the King Bees were doing their best to copy the Beatles and Rolling Stones, and their music sounded very unoriginal. Even though his record failed, David was still convinced that he would be a star someday, and he quit his job as a designer.

British TV producer Barry Langford ruffles David Jones's hair during a publicity stunt.

## New Sounds and a New Look

David would also quit the King Bees a short time later. Looking for a new band in 1965, David wandered into a new group called the Manish Boys, and in no time he and the group were playing shows. There was an explosion of style and fashion that came along with all of the music in

London at this time. Many of the kids were calling themselves "mods," short for modern. The mods went out of their way to dress up, often wearing three-piece suits, ties, and fancy shoes. They were young superconsumers, buying up fashions as soon as they were released and changing to new ones just as quickly. David decided to be a mod. He couldn't afford to shop at the trendiest clothing stores in London, so he went through their garbage bins to find new clothes. He wanted to project the right image as lead singer of this new band. Eventually, "fashion" would be a word that belonged to David Bowie, but in these early days, he had to struggle to find the coolest new clothes.

His always-distinctive hairstyle had continued to change, and his hair was now pretty long. As a publicity stunt for the Manish Boys, David formed the bogus League for the Preservation of Animal Filament, a fancy way of saying "League of Long Hair." In November of 1964, David even went on television in Britain claiming that his "League" was tired of young men with long hair being picked on by the locals. As far as publicity stunts go, this was a pretty silly one, but it did get David on TV.

David's look was always evolving. By his late teens, he was very into "mod" style.

He and the Manish Boys were soon recording again, this time for Parlophone Records, another successful British label. Their song "I Pity the Fool," with a B-side of "Take My Tip," was released on March 5, 1965. Like his previous recording, it was another commercial lemon, selling very few copies.

David was now growing tired of the Manish Boys. He auditioned for another band, the Lower Third. He got the job, and later in 1965, the Lower Third started seeing some small success. David's old bands had been trying to mimic the radio-friendly sounds of the Beatles and the Rolling Stones before, but since that time a new band calling itself the Who was getting hot in England. The Lower Third had a sound that was much closer to that of the Who. Sure enough, David was recording again in the blink of an eye, again for Parlophone, and again without success.

## Becoming David Bowie

It was around this time that Ken Pitt, a businessman and manager who would later become David's manager, had a suggestion for him. He mentioned that there was another Davy Jones who had been performing on the British stage in a musical production of *Oliver!*, and that this other young man was starting to get a lot of press. He told David that he should consider changing his name to something more memorable. Mick Jagger, the singer for the Rolling Stones, had always claimed that the name Jagger meant "knife" in Old English. Since David had always wanted to be like the Stones, and because the letter "b" could stand for Beatles, another group David wanted to mimic, David decided on the name of an American knife that started with a "b." The other Davy Jones would become part of the popular American television series *The Monkees*, and David "Davie" Jones would become David Bowie, after American explorer Jim Bowie's trademark knife.

**1947**
David Robert Jones is born to John and Peggy Jones.

**1964**
David's first-ever recording is released. Davie Jones and the King Bees's single, released by Decca Records, is called "Liza Jane," and has a B-side called "Louie Louie Go Home."

**1969**
On July 20, the United States *Apollo 11* moon-walk mission is launched. On British TV, the moon walk is shown with David Bowie's "Space Oddity" playing in the background, making the first significant impact of his career.

**1971**
In January, David makes his first trip ever to America. On May 28, David's first child, Duncan Zowie Haywood Bowie, is born to him and Angie.

**1973**
David performs as Ziggy Stardust for the first time at the Hammersmith Odeon. By doing so, he opens the doors for all of the new and unusual stage personae he will use in future years.

## 1975

Fame," from the album *Young Americans*, is released. Co-written with John Lennon of the Beatles, it becomes David's first U.S. number-one single.

## 1976

David moves to Berlin and begins work on the trilogy of albums widely regarded by critics to be his most interesting: *Low*, *Heroes*, and *Lodger*.

## 1983

The Serious Moonlight Tour is a huge success. Madison Square Garden schedules a third date after the first two dates sell out.

## 1996

David is inducted into the Rock and Roll Hall of Fame.

## 1997

An all-star concert to celebrate David's fiftieth birthday is held at Madison Square Garden. Modern musicians such as the Smashing Pumpkins play side by side with the influential and respected Bowie.

## 2001

On April 22, David's second child, a daughter, is born to him and Iman. Her name is Alexandria Zahara Jones.

## 2 ✩

## A New Beginning for David Bowie

With his new name came a new confidence, and in January of 1966, a new band. This time his backing group was called the Buzz. Different band, same story: no one was buying any of the music they recorded. It wasn't long before the Buzz was history. It was at this time that David began his career as a solo artist. His new manager, Ken Pitt, was convinced that David could be a superstar of music, movies, musicals, and television. Pitt encouraged David to write solid pop songs that would have wide-ranging appeal for a lot of people. At the same time, David's interest in art was pulling him in a different direction. His hair was even longer now, and he was getting involved in free festivals where people could come to watch rock and roll and poetry without buying tickets. In the late 1960s, with the Vietnam War raging in Southeast Asia, more and more of the kids who had been mods were shedding their interest in fashion and consumerism, and had turned their attention to social and spiritual issues. Called hippies, they protested for peace and freedom, and tried to raise interest in the arts. David was very excited about these new developments, and his style of music was changing to reflect his new interests. He started playing softer music with an acoustic guitar, often sitting on the floor with his legs crossed.

## Solo Sort-of Star

**By the late '60s, David had embraced the trappings of the hippie counterculture.**

David was given his first recording contract as a solo artist by Deram Records, a new company that Decca had started for emerging artists in late 1966. This time, there were no other people for David to share the spotlight with. Any successes he had would be his alone, as would any failures. Deram was planning to release an entire LP this time, not just a single. At this point, David was badly in need of a successful record. He had no real job and was living in his parents' house, but hated every minute of it. He slept at his manager's house whenever he was in London, and eventually moved in with him.

A single from his self-titled solo album, *David Bowie*, was his latest stab at stardom. The single was called "Love You Till Tuesday" and it was another weak seller. After eleven consecutive failures in recording, and no money to show for it, it was clear that David had to change something. His manager and his father tried to convince him to start a cabaret act. A traditional cabaret act is usually made up of a singer performing in a nightclub, singing a number of old popular songs and telling jokes and stories in between. It was the type of performance

## Fun Fact!

When Bowie was studying at Bromley Tech, his art teacher, Owen Frampton, was the father of a classmate who also had a band. The boy, Peter Frampton, was in a band called the Little Ravens at the time, but he would grow up to massive superstardom in the 1970s with his smash-hit live album, *Frampton Comes Alive!*

that appealed to older audiences, and it was not what David really wanted to do, but he needed money and he trusted his manager. After his cabaret act also failed, he got back to doing the things he truly had a passion for.

## The Mime

In 1967, David became friends with a man named Lindsay Kemp. Kemp was the leader of a mime troupe. Mime is a kind of theater where the performers do not talk. They wear white makeup and try to convey meaning and emotion using only their body movements and facial expressions. David joined Kemp's mime troupe and provided music for his performances. A great many of the things David learned during his time in the mime troupe would prove very valuable in the future, as he managed to bring many of these movements into his rock and roll performances.

He was very happy with the artistic things he was pursuing, but David still had no money, and his first full album was now ten months old, a very long time in the fast-moving music business.

Seeing very little future in his career prospects, Deram Records wanted nothing more to do with him. Now he had no money and no record contract. While he was never more confident that he would be a huge star, the rest of the world was starting to doubt the bright future of David Bowie.

He and his manager were looking for a way to save his dying career. David performed any jobs that he could get while they tried to work out a new strategy. He was an extra in a British Broadcasting Corporation (BBC) movie, *The Pistol Shot*, and acted in an ice cream commercial, but he needed something really special to make things happen. It did not take long for them to hatch a new plan.

## Video Visions

David and Ken Pitt decided they would make a movie of songs from David's first album. Keep in mind that this was years before MTV, and the idea of making a "music movie" was strongly original. The movie, to be called *Love You Till Tuesday*, would have David singing songs from his first album and reading some poems, but they wanted something really fresh to cap it all off. To make the movie something memorable, they decided that David should write a brand new song exclusively for the film.

He had recently seen a very important movie, director Stanley Kubrick's *2001: A Space Odyssey*. A wildly original story (based on a book by Arthur C. Clarke), the scenes of space travel and superintelligent computers were like nothing that had ever come before. In later years, it would prove to be a very highly praised and influential film. David could feel a song forming in his brain while he was watching it, but he had no idea exactly what it would be. With the help of John Hutchinson, a former member of his old band the Buzz, he set to work putting his thoughts into sound. After much hard work, the result was a song called "Space Oddity," a clever play on the title of Kubrick's film. "Space Oddity" told the wild, futuristic tale of an astronaut named Major Tom who steps outside of his capsule and decides to float away in space forever. Everyone had a feeling about the song, but they couldn't possibly know at the time what it would mean for David's future.

## A Mirror Image

David was sharing an apartment with Hermione Farthingdale, his girlfriend at the time. When that relationship failed, he was forced to move back to his parents' house. His film, *Love You Till Tuesday*, had proven to be another in a long line of good ideas that went nowhere, and his career was still looking like a no-go. At a time when so little seemed to be working out, his life was about to take an important turn. David was introduced to a young woman named Mary Angela Barnett, known to her friends as Angie. They were instantly attracted to one another, and before long, were completely inseparable and moved in together. Angie provided David with the kind of support that he needed, and she never hesitated to tell him how brilliant she thought he was. Finally, he had met someone who was as confident in his future stardom as he was.

Bowie's future wife, Angie Barnett, sees him off at the train station.

Angie was very interested in fashion. She had her finger on the pulse of style and loved to shop for outrageous new clothes for David.

Additionally, her wild, loud personality helped David break through his own quiet nature and meet important people. They had become best friends very quickly, and it seemed that they were soul mates. David already had his manager, Ken

Pitt, but he trusted his new girlfriend's judgement much more. Unlike so many other musicians' girlfriends, Angie Barnett had an upper-class attitude and education that impressed strangers easily. Her huge vocabulary instantly made her sound intelligent and she had a way of dealing with strangers that made them feel special. Her partnership with David seemed to be exactly what he needed to break new ground in his personal and professional life.

## A Career Takes Flight

David's relationship with Angie was quickly becoming closer. They were truly happy, but David still had zero happening as a musician. The man who would eventually be a rock and roll legend was just a twenty-two-year-old boy with nothing but a string of disappointments to his name. He had written "Space Oddity," and everyone in his camp thought it would be a great success, but he needed someone to let him record it. America had the first walk on the moon planned for July 20, 1969, so it was necessary that they get the song finished and recorded before this important event. Astronauts were hot, so David had to use some of that heat to warm up his own career.

Based on the promise of this new song, Mercury Records struck a deal to record three singles and one full album. David's contract was for one year, with two more one-year options. This gave David another chance at the stardom he'd been waiting for. David's manager called in a favor he was owed by a television executive and was promised that "Space Oddity" would be played during the British television coverage of the American moon landing. Sure enough, when the U.S. astronauts planted the flag, David Bowie's song was playing for all the country to hear.

## Family Farewell

David was attending the Maltese Song Festival, a folk singers' convention in Malta, a short time after the release of "Space Oddity" in July 1969. While there, he received an award for best produced song. It was very exciting, and he returned home to England feeling great, but his triumph would prove to be short-lived. While performing a show, he received a phone call from home. His father, John, was very sick with pneumonia. David rushed home to be by his side, but

The first moon landing was televised in Britain featuring Bowie's "Space Oddity."

John died shortly after. Before John passed away, David showed him his new award. He had always supported and believed in David, and now he was never going to be able to see his son become the success that he always dreamt he would. His father's death made David determined to be as successful as possible.

Five weeks after John's death, and seven weeks after its release, "Space Oddity" made its debut on the British charts. Entering at number thirty-eight, it quickly slipped off, and it looked like David would have to get himself ready for another failure. The song, however, re-entered the charts, and slowly but surely it reached the number eight slot. Finally, David had himself a real hit. He and Angie had been living in his mother's home, but with this new success, they had the freedom to find a place of their own. It was finally looking like David was on his way.

## New Friends

David even had another full album released. Called *David Bowie* in England (the same title as his first) and *Man of Words, Man of Music* in the United States, it was released on November 4, 1969. It was not a big seller, but he started to develop a small cult audience that truly loved his music. Up to this point, he was still playing a kind of folk music, and the British rock scene was mostly dominated by harder rock acts like Led Zeppelin. He needed a collaborator who

Soon after they first met, David Bowie and Mick Ronson became longtime musical collaborators and friends.

had more of a feel for popular rock if he was to break through to a new audience. He met the man who fit that description perfectly when a mutual friend introduced him to Mick Ronson.

Ronson was a hard-rock guitarist with an English accent so thick he could barely be understood. He had been classically trained and knew not only how to play guitar, but how to make complex and beautiful string arrangements. He was a calm and humble man who did not want the spotlight, and was perfect for David because of that. There would be no risk of Ronson trying to upstage him. After meeting Ronson, he put together a new band. David had been singing very sincere songs, and had been showing the world a very down-to-earth face. He decided that his new band would be all about making a scene. They would be all style. He named them the Hype, and at one of their shows, they all dressed up in outrageous, colorful costumes, something David would expand on much more later on.

He had found a new band, and the next steps he took were to get a new manager and a new wife. He and Angie were married on March 20, 1970. At this point in his young life, he had already been through a number of record contracts and bands, but he had still seen so little come of it. Now he seemed to be taking on things with much more permanence. He had a home and a bride now, but he had yet to really make an impact on the music world. At twenty-two years old, there was still a lot of time left for him to find the thing that would take him from being a British folk singer with a small following to a household name.

# 3

## Talent from Another World

David had to keep trying, so he and his band set to work on another album. His new album, *The Man Who Sold the World*, was something new for him in that it relied more on the harder rock experience of Mick Ronson. Whereas many of David's older songs were similar to those of one of his heroes, American folk singer Bob Dylan, this new batch of tunes was darker and heavier.

David's performance style was developing as an odd mix that combined cabaret, folk, hard rock, mime, and complete madness. He had not hit upon the proper formula just yet, but all of the information gathering he did would eventually help him figure out exactly who he was going to be for the public.

*The Man Who Sold the World* did not do any real business in the record stores, but David's small following continued to grow. For every ten critics who dismissed his songs, there was one who fell head over heels in love with them and was willing to tell the world about it. To get the rock critics in America interested in his album, his record company arranged for David to make a promotional tour, visiting with record executives and radio stations to talk about his record. He went all over the country, soaking up all things American. He visited Washington, D.C., San Francisco, Los Angeles, and New York. David loved seeing all of the newest trends in American popular culture, and he was having a lot of fun

**David Bowie poses in his famous "man's dress."**

surprising the stuffy American media by showing up to interviews wearing a dress. He met many important people in the art world and music industry. He began thinking of changing record labels yet again to RCA Records, the label that owned the contract to rock legend Elvis Presley.

## Everything's Hunky Dory

If anything, the trip to America was the perfect time for David to start writing another new batch of songs. All of his influences and ideas were starting to come together, and the things and people he had been exposed to in the United States breathed fresh new life into his music. He was energized. He talked to his new manager,

Tony DeFries, and he encouraged David to keep writing. David gave Mick Ronson a call at his home and asked him to come to London to start working on new music. Ronson brought some of his musician friends with him, and David had himself another new band.

The first project that they began work on was David's next full-length album, *Hunky Dory*. The term "hunky dory" is a slang expression that means everything is great. The title of the album mirrored what was going on in David's life; everything really was great for David at this point. In the middle of all of the craziness, with him and his management trying to get another record deal, and with his band putting together a new album, David and Angela had a son. Duncan Zowie Haywood Bowie was born on May 28, 1971. He was known as Zowie from that moment on, but insisted on being called "Joey" later on. David had a real family of his own to take care of now, and the pressure was on for him to really come through with a huge-selling album.

He had been doing a lot of work for *Hunky Dory*, but a seed that he had planted in his

45

# Terry's Illness

David's older brother, Terry, had been diagnosed as having schizophrenia, a mental illness that both his grandmother and his aunt had. This meant that Terry's personality was never the same from one minute to the next. He could be very kind and supportive one minute, and then be angry or not say anything at all the next. He had disappeared from home for various periods of time, and had been found by the police wandering around, unsure of where he was. A lot of the material on *The Man Who Sold the World* dealt with Terry and David's feelings about Terry's illness. Terry was living in mental hospitals on and off, and was never the same person when visited.

David's family's history of mental illness was something that he was very afraid of. He used this worry to his advantage by writing about it. In many ways, it could be said that writing and performing music kept him sane. Like so many of the other experiences in his life, he would collect his meetings with Terry in his memory and find a way to spin them into musical gold.

mind earlier was starting to grow into a full-fledged idea, and he was trying to work on that at the same time. It would be a concept album about a rock star, and David and his band would play a fictional band. He did not have a lot of the details worked out, but this project was going to be the one that perfectly combined all of the personas David Bowie had been before. First, though, he had to finish *Hunky Dory*.

## Many Changes

In November 1971, the RCA deal was finally sealed, and *Hunky Dory* was completed and released. Its sound was yet another different direction for David, with the hard rock of *The Man Who Sold the World* softened and prettied by pianos and pop. It was his most likeable record yet, and almost everyone could agree

### Fun Fact!

On a trip to New York, David met one of his heroes, the hugely famous pop artist Andy Warhol. Warhol had recently become very famous because of a series of paintings of Campbell's Soup cans, and pieces of art inspired by popular stars like Elvis and Marilyn Monroe. He was so impressed by the artist, in fact, that he wrote a song for *Hunky Dory* called "Andy Warhol."

that he was starting to become a strong songwriter. The record company released a single from the album, called "Changes." The leadoff song, it was a near-perfect pop song in which he declared his new direction. The song and the album were not big sellers at the time, but did fair business, certainly better than any of his

**Bowie poses in his "Lauren Bacall" getup during the *Hunky Dory* era.**

previous records. Many of the music business insiders he had met on both coasts of the United States were spreading the word about him. The number of people in Los Angeles and New York who knew about David Bowie grew every second.

Many of the mainstream music critics were still not quite ready for David then, and while he received some bright notices for the album, it was not totally accepted yet. Interestingly enough, *Hunky Dory* would grow to become a favorite album of many young musicians today, and is considered a classic. It was even chosen as one of the 100 greatest albums in rock by music video channel VH-1, in a list made up by musicians and producers. To David and his crew, the fact that *Hunky Dory* was not a big success at the time was quickly forgotten. They had something even better up their sleeves. The idea that had been growing in David's head was ready to burst out, and it would be the birth of this brand new image that would finally put him over the top.

## The Star on Earth

A concept album is a type of record that the Beatles had pioneered. On a concept album, all of the songs come together to tell a story. Pop music and rock and roll had started out as art forms based on releasing singles, and the full-length LPs released were usually just a loose collection of singles. When the Beatles released

*Sgt. Pepper's Lonely Hearts Club Band,* the entire album told a story that unfolded during the songs. The songs were played by the Beatles, but they pretended to be another band that did not really exist. It was a sensational smash hit for them, and it truly changed the face of rock and roll. Now it was David's turn to try to change things. His idea was similar; his new record would tell a story and be played by a fictional band that was really he and his band, but that's where the similarities ended. David was about to create something that the world had never before seen.

Throughout his career, David had always been playing roles. He had been a young saxophone hero, a folk singer, a hard rocker, a pop singer, a mime, a hippie, a mod; he had even been a man in a dress! This time, he would be an alien. His newest character was a strange man named Ziggy Stardust. Ziggy's story was that he was from another planet, and had come to Earth to form a band called the Spiders from Mars. He and his band became huge stars, and then the pressures of the rock and roll lifestyle destroyed him. The story would unfold over the course of eleven songs.

This was a project where David was using everything that he had experienced in his young life to its fullest. He was taking his brother's split personalities to create his own other personality. He was using the makeup and hand motions of his experience as a mime. He was taking the outrageous, brightly colored styles of American pop culture and using them in his own way. He was also taking the best parts of his own past recordings, especially the schizophrenia of *The Man Who Sold the World* and the science fiction of "Space Oddity," to make something new.

While the subjects of the songs were new, and the concept was different, the actual music would be more of a return to his harder rocking days. David was through writing and playing folk songs and was thinking more about style. He was, in part, returning to the days of his band, the Hype, and even had Mick Ronson around to influence this new sound. The new music would be loud and heavy, and, most of all, it would be huge.

He had a lot of the details for this new project worked out, but something important was still missing. He needed a new look. He wanted to look like nothing that had ever been seen before. His style was usually based on the current trends; even the feminine "man's dress" that he wore to shock the press was worn first by the singer of the Rolling Stones, Mick Jagger. Now, though, he needed something really shocking.

## Man or Space Man?

David had a naturally unusual look. He was always very thin and had eyes and limbs that made him look not quite human. He had the kind of look that made it sometimes hard to tell if he was a man or a woman, and he had been using that to make people take interest in his strange ways. His hair was very long now, but that was nothing new. So he talked about it with Angie and his stylist, and by looking at European fashion magazines they cooked up a look that was totally original.

David's bizarre new hairstyle was short and spiky on the top, already a very different

**Sporting a provocative new hairstyle, Bowie is shown during the tour with the Spiders from Mars.**

look from many modern long-haired rockers, and long and feathery in the back. Not completely satisfied with the style, they went even further by dyeing it a bright, fire-engine red, a shade that no real human could ever have. He also shaved off his eyebrows, helping along the idea that he was not a human being. Finally, he had his stylist create a series of expensive costumes that looked nothing like normal human clothes.

He was ready to introduce the world to his creation from another world. He and his Spiders from Mars began playing shows. The audiences were stunned by his strange look and the futuristic, gold costumes worn by the band. He almost seemed like some kind of comic-book character come to life. The songs were the best he had ever done. The combination of the pop polish he had played with on *Hunky Dory* and the heavy rock of *The Man Who Sold the World*, put together and packaged in this new, shiny wrapping, created the perfect formula that he had been searching for. The demand for his new album, called *The Rise and Fall of Ziggy Stardust and the Spiders from Mars*, was growing, and suddenly the world that had never cared about his work wanted to know who this amazing man was.

The album was released on March 2, 1972, and the praise came quickly. The critics agreed for the first time that David Bowie was someone to watch very closely, and his fan base was no longer just in small pockets. Ziggy Stardust and the Spiders from Mars were filling up concert venues and the record was starting to jump off the shelves. Ever since his high school days of putting an orange streak in his hair, David had known that appearance and style were everything, but he had not known just what kind of appearance would work. It was like the completion of his training.

Soon, his manager was getting calls from American booking agents saying they wanted David to play their ballrooms, theaters, and nightclubs. To make it big in America was any musician's dream. It was the birthplace of rock and roll, and American artists were thought of as the biggest trendsetters of the day. For David to crack the U.S. market would be a gigantic feat, and the fact that people were starting to show interest was a good sign.

## The Next Big Thing

Meanwhile, back in England, *The Rise and Fall of Ziggy Stardust and the Spiders from Mars* was a top

Bowie rocks out in another strange costume during the tour following the release of *Ziggy Stardust*.

ten hit. The Bowie camp's plan for stardom was
very simple. If people were going to believe that
David was a star, he was going to start living like a
star. Suddenly, only the finest hotels would do.
David and Angie started traveling by limousine.
In interviews, he spoke brilliantly about how
important his music was and told the world that
he was the next big thing. The plan was working.
By telling people that he was not a young,
unproven musician, but a gigantic star, even
though he was still a young, unproven musician,
they believed him and paid much closer
attention to his music. This was the way to do
things if he was to succeed in the United States.

Bowie's management did not waste any time
planning an American tour. Called U.S. Tour
One, it was difficult to organize because of David's
fear of heights and flying. The first date of the
tour was in the middle of the country, in
Cleveland, Ohio. It was easy to get towns like Los
Angeles or New York on your side if you are an
emerging musician, but it's much more difficult to
capture the imagination of the more conservative
parts of the country. If David failed in Cleveland, it

would not look good for his immediate future as a performer in the United States. It did not take long for everyone to figure out that playing Cleveland was not going to be a problem. Immediately upon arriving at Cleveland Music Hall, David was met by thousands of fans dressed up like Ziggy Stardust. The 3,500-seat auditorium was sold out. It was clear that America belonged to David Bowie if he wanted it.

He went on to play New York's famous Carnegie Hall, as well as shows in Boston, and two sold-out shows in a row in Los Angeles. His old contacts in the music business from his early visits to L.A. had never stopped talking him up to the press and to their friends, and his audience there was his largest. While some of the shows had a lower attendance than expected, it was understood that David Bowie and his Ziggy Stardust had arrived.

He was not satisfied to stop there, though. His team quickly organized another tour of the United States, a tour of Japan, and a welcome-home tour of England. David was especially excited about the Japanese tour, as he had also borrowed from the

Ziggy Stardust and the Spiders from Mars perform at London's famous Hammersmith Odeon.

traditional Japanese theater art of Kabuki (in which the performers wear white makeup and make dramatic hand motions). He was hot and now was the time to strike. He was selling lots of tickets, but he was spending more money than he was making, so he really needed to keep touring to make up for it. If the illusion that he was a wealthy superstar was to continue, he needed the money to do it. So he stayed on the road.

## A Lad, Insane

He was still working hard to make it in the United States, but in England he had already arrived. His next album, *Aladdin Sane,* was greeted by advance sales of 100,000 copies. This was the largest advance sales number since the mighty Beatles themselves. David had written many of the songs while on the road in America, and the album was rushed in order to cash in quickly. He had listed the names of the American cities in which each song had been written, and it was believed that this was another concept album, this time one about modern

America. Because the press had gotten used to him playing characters, they began labeling his new character "Aladdin Sane," after the album's title. They liked the clever play on words. Ziggy Stardust had risen and fallen, and now he was "A Lad, Insane."

The record spent eight weeks at number one on the British charts, and he had three top-ten hit singles, "Jean Genie," "Drive in Saturday," and "Life on Mars," a track from *Hunky Dory*. In fact, at this time, he was so popular in England that many songs from his older, less popular albums were automatically going top ten. Deram Records even released "The Laughing Gnome," one of his earliest songs, and it also went top ten. It looked like this Aladdin had some kind of magic lantern, because everything he wished for was coming true.

David continued touring like mad, and while he was steadily gaining fame in the United States, he was still not selling as many tickets as he wanted. Exhausted from all the touring and in need of a publicity stunt that would cause high demand for his music, he and his management cooked up a new scheme. He was set to play the Hammersmith Odeon, a British concert hall, for the finale of his British tour on July 3, 1973. When he arrived at the date, everything seemed fine, but toward the end of the show, he announced to the audience that this would be his last show ever. He said he was retiring from performing. He had not even told his band about this surprise, and they were just as shocked as his audience. He believed that if he didn't appear for a while, the demand for his music would build up to the point where he could automatically sell out any American or British arena. At that time, he would begin touring again.

## It's Covered

In the meantime, he set to work on a quick and fun exercise that would help ease some tension from all the touring and publicity. His next album was going to be a cover album. By performing a group of songs that had been made famous by other, more recognizable musicians, he would be reaching out to the audiences that preferred "oldies," and showing respect to the artists whose music he had grown up on.

Called *Pin-Ups*, the album featured covers of old songs by British rock acts like the Who and the Kinks. It was nothing new, but it had the same results of a master painter doing a quick comic strip, and it renewed David's energy. He would be ready now to start something that was much larger and more serious.

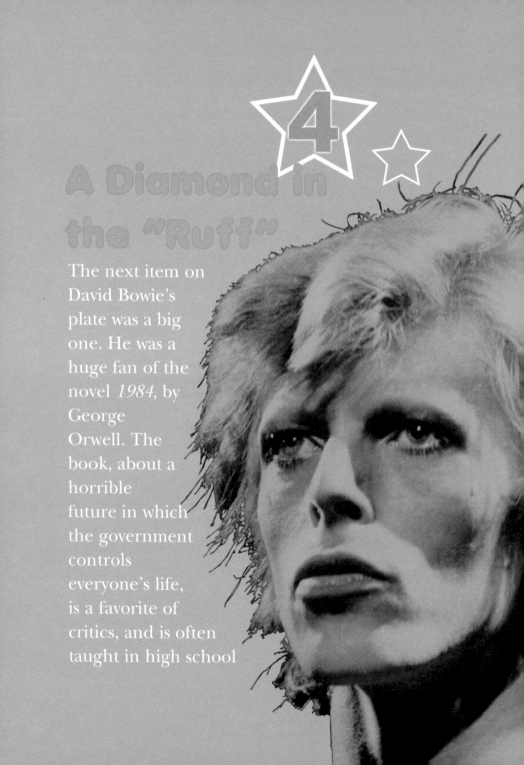

## 4

## A Diamond in the "Ruff"

The next item on David Bowie's plate was a big one. He was a huge fan of the novel *1984*, by George Orwell. The book, about a horrible future in which the government controls everyone's life, is a favorite of critics, and is often taught in high school

English classes. David wanted to make a musical version of the story. This original plan ran into some problems, however. George Orwell's widow did not want David to do the musical and refused to give her permission. Because of that, the project turned into another concept album only loosely based on *1984*.

Called *Diamond Dogs* after a line from the book, it was another hard-rocking album that borrowed a lot from the rough rhythm and blues of the Rolling Stones. David was starting to get interested in the soul music sounds from the United States, and this was also coming out in his music. The album was released on June 1, 1974, along with a single one week before, called "Rebel Rebel." *Diamond Dogs* was another instant success in the United Kingdom.

His management had planned another tour of the United States and Canada, and since it was his return to live performing after "retiring," it was to be his biggest tour yet. Stretching across twenty-three cities, it was more than just a musician playing his songs. It was a real show, with a complicated background and full band with backup singers. It would start in Montreal, Canada, and the first half would end in New York City. Then, after five weeks off, the second half would begin in Los Angeles. For the production, David wanted to develop his vision of a future city like the one in *1984*, so the set for the show was made up to look like a huge, decaying metropolis. The tour was called the Year of the Diamond Dogs.

David continued to incorporate his old influences into his music. He was still obsessed with science fiction and the future, and his look was changing to bring in some of his past. Just as he had once dressed in suits as a young mod, he stopped wearing outrageous space costumes, and instead switched to handsome European tailored suits. It turned out that he had retired after the show at the Hammersmith Odeon, in a way. He had retired Ziggy Stardust. David Bowie, on the other hand, had a few more performances left in him. And a new face. He was calling his new look and character "Halloween Jack."

The show opened to big business all over the United States. People were stunned by the spectacular new show, and even though some fans wanted Ziggy Stardust back, many were just as interested in his new style. During the tour, something he had been waiting for forever finally happened. Both *Diamond Dogs* and *The Rise and Fall of Ziggy Stardust* went gold in America. He had finally sold enough copies of his records to be considered a major star. His dream had become a reality.

## The Sigma Sound

While on tour, David spent some time at

69

Philadelphia's Sigma Sound Studio. Sigma was known as the place where hit soul records were pumped out as if from an assembly line. David was impressed with their track record, and liked the smooth, slick, radio-friendly sound of Philly Soul. After visiting, he decided that he wanted to make his next album there, and that he would start working more soul into his musical blend. He believed that if he was going to kidnap the ears of America, he had to lure them to him with a sound that was pure U.S.A. The answer, it seemed, was the Sigma sound.

He had been scouting out new musicians to work with for his new sound, and he had been very impressed by a funk musician named Carlos Alomar, a member of a band called the Main Ingredient. He wanted Carlos to be his musical director, as Mick Ronson had once done before going solo. He also met a soul singer named Luther Vandross. A childhood friend of Alomar's, it only took seconds of singing to convince David that Luther should be working with him.

Even though he was still in the middle of his tour, David's new full album was planned. It

Bowie debuted yet another original look during the tour for the *Diamond Dogs* album, released in 1974.

would be called *Young Americans,* which made it clear who David was aiming his new music at. Because he was already so ready to do something new, he quickly lost interest in all of the complications of the Diamond Dogs tour. He told his crew that for the second half of the tour, there would be no more sets and props. Just a simple white backdrop, and he was going to start working more of his new songs into the playlist.

He was in love with the city of Los Angeles, which he called his "favorite museum," and while he was staying there during the tour he met and became friends with such huge celebrities as John Lennon of the Beatles and movie goddess Elizabeth Taylor. After the tour, he would make L.A. his home. Bowie was about to shift gears again, and in Los Angeles, another piece of the puzzle of his career was about to be filled in.

## 5

## The Thin White Duke in Berlin

Bowie eventually finished *Young Americans*, but there was one last little detail to clear up. He decided that he wanted to record a John Lennon song for the end of the album, and invited Lennon to the sessions for recording. While Lennon was there, he and Carlos Alomar accidentally stumbled upon a near-perfect guitar riff and developed it. David liked what he heard and wrote some lyrics quickly. The song became "Fame." Co-written with his teen idol from the Beatles, it would become David Bowie's first American number-one hit.

Now that David had a number-one hit, no one was questioning the fact that he was one of the world's biggest pop stars, but he was having money troubles. His management deal had made it so that he was not getting much of the money that he deserved for his music, so he decided to change managers. It was a difficult process, but he got out of his old contract and was in charge of his own career for the first time. He had always been playing roles in his music, but he was itching now for the chance to play a role in the movies. His chance was about to come.

## The Man Who Fell To Earth

Nicholas Roeg, a young underground film director who had worked with Mick Jagger, was searching for a star for his next project. The film was to be called *The Man Who Fell to Earth,* and would be about an alien who left his planet in order to find a way to stop a drought from killing everyone on it. After seeing a documentary about him on British television, Roeg knew that David was the star he needed for his movie. David agreed to do the film and packed up for Los Angeles.

Much of the filming took place in New Mexico, far from the star power and glamour of Hollywood, and it was the perfect place for David to really work on his performance. This was a man who had first made a music career out of playing an alien, and

**Bowie played a space alien in the 1976 film *The Man Who Fell to Earth*.**

now he was trying to make a movie career out of playing one. He was always on time to the set and never complained about the complicated makeup he had to have applied every day. He spent his free time painting and drawing, and seemed happy to get away from the glitz of being a celebrity.

The film was released to mostly good reviews, and David's performance was widely considered a good one. It was a strange film, though, and did not do a lot of business. Years later, it would go on to become a cult classic, and is now considered an excellent piece of modern science fiction. Overall, the experience was a positive one, and it proved that David could work in a film.

## Station to Stadium

David had been asked to work on music for the soundtrack of *The Man Who Fell to Earth,* and he did for a while, but he was so busy and overworked that he had to stop. He had planned a tour, though, to publicize the music and the movie, so he began recording a new studio album instead. This new album would be called *Station to Station* and would take the soul and funk of *Young Americans* and twist it with very modern electronic and disco sounds that were starting to gain popularity in American and European dance clubs.

The album gave him another hit single, the top ten "Golden Years." David was also planning his first world tour. For the tour and album, he

For the tour following the release of *Station to Station*, Bowie created the well-dressed, yet cold, persona of the Thin White Duke.

created another new character to play: the Thin White Duke. This new character was a cold, stylish man in black and white. For the tour, David tried to look like a performer in an old, silent German movie. The set was all black, and the only lights were strong, bright, white lights that almost seemed solid in the air. As colorful as Ziggy Stardust had been, the Duke was colorless.

For the tour, David had reunited with his old friend (and father of punk rock) Iggy Pop. He and Iggy had both been living in Los Angeles, and they had both started taking drugs. David hated what it was doing to him, so when the tour was finished, he packed up his bags and he and Iggy moved away. He said good-bye to the drugs before they destroyed his life and said good-bye to L.A. along with it.

## Walled in Berlin

David and Iggy, along with David's assistant Coco Schwab and David's son Zowie, moved to Berlin, Germany. David was tired of fame and celebrity and wanted to return to just making music. He started by producing records for Iggy. On them, he worked on and tested some of his own ideas that he wanted to use on his next album. He was interested in working with a musician named Brian Eno, who had futuristic plans for using electronic sound in rock and roll music.

**David hangs out in Berlin with rocker Iggy Pop, one of his best friends.**

David and Eno worked together for three new albums. Called *Low, Heroes,* and *Lodger,* they are thought of by many rock critics as the most interesting of David's career. *Low,* released in 1977, was the first. It was not only a new sound for David, but also for the world. The first half was strange, new, funky electro-pop, with robotic sounds mixed in with David's lyrics. The second half was mostly instrumental. David only sang some harmonies.

# Did You Know?

**During Iggy Pop's tour for his album *The Idiot*, David was just a simple piano and keyboard player. He was often unlit during the performances, and many people did not even know he was there.**

*Heroes*, also from 1977, follows the same weird formula, with the second half of the album all instrumental. Neither album produced any hit songs for David, but his tours were still selling very well, and he was so satisfied with the artistic side of the music that it's failure to sell did not matter. Also, a few years down the line, the kind of electronic pop that he had innovated would dominate the radio, with the electro-dance pop of bands like Duran Duran getting all the airplay.

The third album, *Lodger*, had lyrics for every song, but it was still very unusual and continued to

toy with the electronics of the last two albums.
Again, there were no hits from it, but something
new was starting to happen. One new thing that
record companies were doing was making music
videos. Keep in mind that this was 1979, two years
before MTV. David had already made a film of his
music back in the 1960s, *Love You Till Tuesday*, and
he was eager to try it again. He made three videos
for songs from *Lodger*, and once MTV started, they
aired often. He was one step ahead of everyone
else in the music video game, and that would turn
out to be one of his smartest moves yet.

The time he spent in Berlin would prove to be
very good for David. He had started dressing very
simply, like a German commoner, and he was
riding a bicycle everywhere he went. His marriage
to Angie was failing, but he had much more time
to spend with his son, and for the first time he
could really be a father to him. He continued
painting and drawing, and even had the time to
film a European movie called *Just a Gigolo*. On
January 8, 1980, he turned thirty-three years old.
He had proven everything that he needed to and it
was time for him to get to know himself better.

**6**

Set for Stardom

David Bowie
started the
1980s by
divorcing
Angie. They had
been spending less
and less time together
and there was nothing
left to do but make
their separation legal.
He did not let it ruin his
work ethic, though, and
recorded yet another album,
his fourteenth. *Scary Monsters
(and Super Creeps)* was his
attempt to win back some of the

pop audience that he lost thanks to the electronic experiments on his last three records. It still had a futuristic edge, but a lot of the strange sounds were contained with more of a pop feel. It went to number twelve on the U.S. pop charts, and proved that David was no washed-up ex-rocker.

David had also recently gotten an interesting offer to play the part of the Elephant Man on Broadway in New York City. A very successful play, *The Elephant Man* was a true story about a young man in England who was born with horrible deformities. The elephant man wore a bag on his head and was picked on by everyone he met until a kind doctor decided to help him. The role was very emotionally demanding, even for a very experienced actor. Whoever played him would have no makeup, just their own facial expressions and body. Even though the Elephant Man is supposed to be severely deformed, the director of the play decided that the actor would have to play the role with a bare face and show the deformities through simple acting.

# David Bowie

An audience applauds Bowie and his costars Concetta Tomei and Ken Ruta after a performance of *The Elephant Man*.

While the producers were a little nervous to cast a rock star, they decided to give David a try. It turned out that he was perfect for the part, and when he appeared on Broadway, the reviews of his performance were incredible. David Bowie had conquered music and movies, and now he had the theater. In his five-week run in the play, there was never an empty seat.

## Did You Know?

In 1983, David launched the Serious Moonlight Tour. His greatest touring success yet, the tour forced a third date at New York's famous Madison Square Garden after the first two sold out.

# New Wave Dave

David had been laying low for a while, trying out different music and seeing what he could do with the theater, but he could not wait to get back to the business of recording hit albums. He had to wait until 1983, when his old record contract was up, to record and tour again. What he had planned was something huge. He was ready, after having so much of his money kept from him by his old managers, to release an album that would make him very, very rich. He had done art and theater, but now he wanted to do hits, big hits.

**Bowie and the band jam out onstage during the Serious Moonlight Tour in 1983.**

His entry into the world of MTV and 1980s new-wave music was *Let's Dance.* It was his first album under his new contract with EMI/Capitol Records—the contract that had just made him millions of dollars. The album was, in some ways, the perfect combination of the pop/soul of *Young Americans* and a modern funk sound. It was his sleekest, most commercial record yet. He also continued to seek out talented musicians to work with, this time finding the amazing blues guitarist Stevie Ray Vaughn.

By 1983, music videos had become the wave of the future. Bowie had always been a visual artist who was at his best when he was seen and heard. He already had a head start with videos from *Lodger* and *Scary Monsters,* but he had a whole new image to show the public for *Let's Dance.* The new David was tan, very blond, and always wore a sharp suit and tie. He looked every bit the rich man that he wanted this new record to make him. While he was putting on a new, very acceptable and commercial face, many of the other pop stars of the day seemed to be stealing his old look, with makeup-wearing hitmakers like Culture Club making people wonder whether they were men or women. At the dawn of the eighties, just how important David Bowie had been to music was starting to show.

The album was number four in the United States, and three singles, "Let's Dance," "Modern Love," and "China Girl," were giant American hits. After a slow period in his career, David

# David Bowie

Bowie was once again one of the rock world's biggest stars. Because of his renewed exposure on television and radio, a whole new group of young fans began to buy David's albums and rediscover someone that their parents and older siblings had been brought up listening to. Despite so many years in the music business, he somehow managed to keep himself new. There would, however, be new frontiers for David Bowie to cross before he was finished.

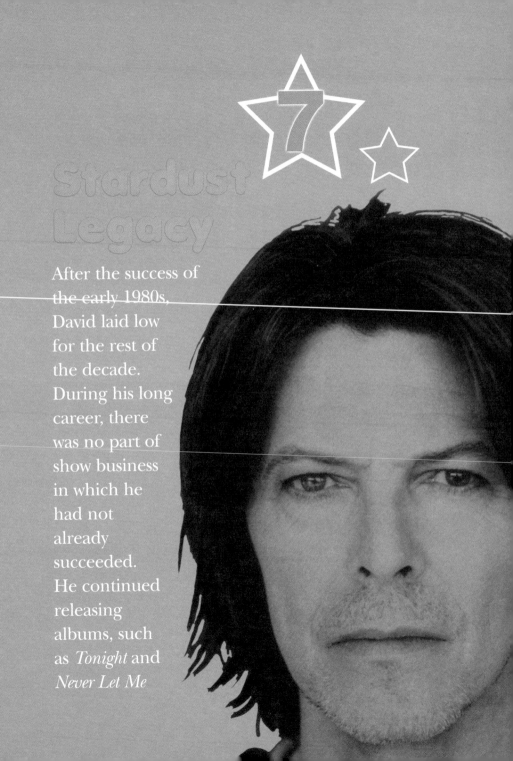

# 7

## Stardust Legacy

After the success of the early 1980s, David laid low for the rest of the decade. During his long career, there was no part of show business in which he had not already succeeded. He continued releasing albums, such as *Tonight* and *Never Let Me*

**Bowie was lauded for his role as Andy Warhol in Julian Schnabel's *Basquiat*.**

*Down.* He also appeared in more movies, like the fantasy adventure *Labyrinth* and legendary director Martin Scorsese's *The Last Temptation of Christ.* He finally had the kind of financial security that would allow him to relax a little and do the things that interested him.

He had become a respected father figure for the entire new generation of British rockers like the Cure and Billy Idol, who would use some of his many looks and sounds in their flashy music videos. It seemed that no matter where you looked, David's enormous shadow fell. Even though he was being looked at as a legend from rock's past, however, he was still a man in his thirties, and he wasn't content to just sit back and watch the world pass him by. Bowie made his

Bowie's second marriage, this one to supermodel Iman, has been going strong since they wed in 1992.

career by being at the height of the cutting edge,
and he wanted to continue.

He began the 1990s by doing another stylistic
about-face and starting a new rock and roll band.
Called Tin Machine, it was the first time since
the Buzz (back in 1966) that David was part of a
band, and not a solo artist. It featured members
of Iggy Pop's band, and the sound was close to
Iggy's. The heavy, grungy rock did not connect
well with the public, but it refreshed David's
creativity and got him ready to continue his solo
career with renewed energy.

Another new development at the beginning of
the '90s was David's second marriage. In 1992, he
married the beautiful Somalian supermodel
Iman. The two have been inseparable ever since
and are still married to this day. The tall, elegant
Iman seems the perfect mate for the man who
made glamour his trademark. "I have someone
who loves me for me," David said. "Seriously, it
really helps."

And the records continued. In the later half
of the '90s, David brought back the electronic
innovations he had helped to introduce the

world to in the late '70s. Since that time, dance and techno music have grown and splintered into entirely new forms, and many of their performers are quick to cite David as a chief influence. One of the most popular electronic performers, Trent Reznor of Nine Inch Nails, has worked with Bowie and appeared in his videos.

**Bowie has collaborated with modern musicians like Trent Reznor of Nine Inch Nails.**

In 1996, David was inducted into the Rock and Roll Hall of Fame. The Rock and Roll Hall of Fame Foundation chooses a select number of performers each year to be inducted, and for David, this was a huge honor. He had been performing and making music for so many years that his influence on rock and roll was undeniable. And as his fiftieth birthday was approaching, it was about to be made even more clear.

Artists from all over the musical map, such as Sonic Youth and Lou Reed, came to perform with him for his giant fiftieth birthday concert at New York's Madison Square Garden in January 1997. Even one of the world's biggest rock groups, U2, was sneaking lyrics from David's "Young Americans" into their songs on their 2001 tour. As if that wasn't enough to prove his importance, the British rock magazine *New Musical Express* recently held a poll of rock musicians in which he was named the number-one most influential musician of all time. Plus, he is a member of the Rock and Roll Hall of Fame. It does not get any clearer than that.

## Starman Launches in Cyberspace

But still there was more for David to conquer. He made himself the first true musician/businessman when on January 31, 1997, he established himself as a publicly owned company. That means that any person with a little cash can buy stocks and bonds that insure the owner a piece of a rock legend's career! It was a shocking move, and it paid off in the amount of $55 million for David right away. Not only was he getting involved in the world of high finance, but he was reaching out a hand and bringing his fans along with him.

Bowie was also one of the first artists to see the true potential of the Internet. On September 1, 1998, he launched his own Web site, BowieNet (http://www.davidbowie.com). Not just a site devoted to his rock triumphs, it is a full Internet service provider (ISP) with e-mail and Web access, and it contains links to his music and art, and audio clips. It even contains a special feature where people visiting the site can help him write the lyrics for a song. As of September 1996, even before he started the site, he was the third most popular male solo artist on the World Wide Web. Since the launch, many other high-profile musicians have followed suit, but once again David Bowie was well ahead of the pack, proving his incredible instincts have not dulled with age.

Billy Corgan of the Smashing Pumpkins joined Bowie onstage for Bowie's fiftieth birthday extravaganza.

# David Bowie

# Did You Know?

Many of the musicians who got their start working with David Bowie went on to achieve massive success on their own. Luther Vandross had a number of solo hit records in the 1980s and 1990s, and the late guitarist Stevie Ray Vaughn is considered a blues legend.

## The Man of Tomorrow, Today

Although in his mid-fifties, David Bowie shows no signs of quitting. He and his wife, Iman, have settled permanently in New York City, where David continues to paint and write songs. Not satisfied resting on his past accomplishments, he has yet another new album coming out, called *Toy*. He also recorded a song with techno innovators Massive Attack for the film *Moulin Rouge*, which starred Nicole Kidman.

He can certainly afford to take it easy if he desires, though. In January 2001, it was revealed that the man who had once had to fight his management to be paid properly for his music was ranked number 257 among British millionaires. This put him right alongside Rolling Stones guitarist Keith Richards, a musician who got a much earlier start than David.

Money is not everything, though. On April 2, 2001, David's mother, Peggy Jones, passed away. She had been living in a nursing home in England and was in her late eighties. The tragedy of the loss of his mother, however, was balanced out by a wonderful event. Later the same month, on April 22, Iman gave birth to a daughter, Alexandria Zahara Jones. She is the second child for both of them, though their first together. It seems that no matter what, life goes on.

## The Legend

David Bowie has experienced success as a musician, actor, painter, Broadway star, Internet pioneer, and captain of finance. He has mastered so many different roles in his long, exciting career, but has somehow managed to remain true to himself. He began life as poor David Jones from a shabby part of England and gradually rose to the rank of rock and roll legend. Today, he stands as one of the most highly regarded musicians in the history of rock and roll, not to mention one of the richest. His influence and contributions to the art form cannot be ignored, and the biggest names in the music business will readily admit that he is a hero. "The Man Who Fell to Earth" is still one of our brightest stars, and he will continue to shine.

# SELECTED DISCOGRAPHY

**1967** *David Bowie*

**1971** *The Man Who Sold the World*

**1971** *Hunky Dory*

**1972** *The Rise and Fall of Ziggy Stardust and the Spiders from Mars*

**1973** *Aladdin Sane*

**1974** *Diamond Dogs*

**1975** *Young Americans*

**1977** *Low*

**1977** *Heroes*

**1979** *Lodger*

**1980** *Scary Monsters (and Super Creeps)*

**1983** *Let's Dance*

**1987** *Never Let Me Down*

**1989** *Tin Machine I*

**1997** *Earthling*

**1999** *Hours*

# SELECTED FILMOGRAPHY

1969 *The Virgin Soldiers*

1976 *The Man Who Fell to Earth*

1979 *Just a Gigolo*

1981 *Wir Kinder von Bahnhof Zoo (Christiane F.)*

1983 *The Hunger*

1983 *Merry Christmas, Mr. Lawrence*

1983 *Yellowbeard*

1983 *Ziggy Stardust and the Spiders from Mars* (concert movie)

1985 *Into the Night*

1986 *Absolute Beginners*

1986 *Labyrinth*

1988 *The Last Temptation of Christ*

1991 *The Linguini Incident*

1992 *Twin Peaks: Fire Walk with Me*

1996 *Basquiat*

1999 *Everybody Loves Sunshine*

2000 *Mr. Rice's Secret*

# GLOSSARY

**cabaret** A nightclub act that involves jokes, storytelling, and singing famous old standards.

**collaborator** A partner with whom someone works on a project.

**concept album** A record that, instead of being a loose collection of singles, uses every song together to tell a story.

**consumerism** The desire to spend money on mass-marketed products.

**cult audience** A small, very loyal fan base that supports a largely unknown performer.

**documentary** A non-fiction film that focuses on the life of one true-life subject.

**futuristic** Something that is ahead of its time; appearing to be from a time that has not yet happened.

**guise** Outward appearance; a way of dressing or behaving.

**image** The way someone is seen by the public.

**individuality**  Being different than others.

**inductees**  People who are about to be entered into an exclusive club or organization.

**influential**  When a person or a work of art has left a lasting impact on people or works that have come after it.

**Kabuki**  A form of Japanese theater that involves white makeup and grand hand gestures and body language.

**metropolis**  A large, highly developed and populated city.

**mods**  A group of English young people during the 1960s who were interested in fashion and rock and roll.

**musical director**  A musician in charge of arranging all of the instruments in an artist's band.

**pneumonia**  A disease that affects the lungs and breathing, and can sometimes be fatal.

**pop culture**  Relating to things that are popular or recognized as having mass appeal.

**producer**  A person who is responsible for recording and putting together an album.

**schizophrenia** A mental disorder that makes a person have wild mood swings and occasional hallucinations and delusions.

**sensation** A cause of excitement.

**techno** A type of popular music that relies heavily on electronically created sounds.

**ukulele** A four-string guitar of Portuguese origin, which is smaller than a regular guitar.

**venue** A place where concerts are performed.

# TO FIND OUT MORE

Rock and Roll Hall of Fame and Museum
One Key Plaza
Cleveland, OH 44114
(888) 764-ROCK (7625)
Web site: http://www.rockhall.com

Rock and Roll Hall of Fame Foundation
1290 Avenue of the Americas
New York, NY 10104

## Web Sites

BowieNet v2.0—The Official David Bowie Web site
http://www.davidbowie.com

David Bowie Wonderworld
http://www.bowiewonderworld.com

Teenage Wildlife—A David Bowie Fan Page
http://www.teenagewildlife.com

# FOR FURTHER READING

Buckley, David. *David Bowie.* New York: Omnibus Press, 1996.

Paytress, Mark. *The Rise and Fall of Ziggy Stardust and the Spiders from Mars: David Bowie.* New York: Music Sales Corporation, 2000.

Sandford, Christopher. *Bowie: Loving the Alien.* New York: Da Capo Press, 1998.

Tremlett, George. *David Bowie: Living on the Brink.* New York: Carroll & Graf Publishers, Inc., 1997.

## Works Cited

Edwards, Henry, and Tony Zanetta. *Stardust: The David Bowie Story.* New York: McGraw-Hill, 1986.

Hauptfuhrer, Fred. "Rock's Space Oddity, David Bowie, Falls to Earth and Lands on His Feet in Film." *People*, September 6, 1976.

Wild, David. "Bowie's Wedding Album." *Rolling Stone*, January 21, 1993.

# INDEX

# Index

# CREDITS

## About the Author

Thomas Forget is an author, illustrator, and book designer who lives in New York City.

## Photo Credits

Cover, p. 89 © Reuters Newmedia, Inc./Corbis; pp. 4, 42 © S.I.N./Corbis; pp. 5, 13, 73, 86 © Neal Preston/Corbis; p. 6 © Denis O'Reagan/Corbis; pp. 9, 19, 26, 34, 44, 60–61, 79 © Hulton Archive by Getty Images, Inc.; pp. 21, 28, 37, 39, 49, 54, 57, 66, 71, 77 © Michael Ochs Archive; p. 75 © Corbis; p. 82 © Roger Ressmeyer/Corbis; p. 84 © Lynn Goldsmith/Corbis; pp. 90, 91, 93, 96–97 © Mitchell Gerber/Corbis.

## Layout and Design

Thomas Forget